GOD'S INTERACTIONS

*Some perceivable works
of the Triune God
in the life of a modern-day servant*

THE EARLY YEARS
of L.S. BIGGS

THE WAY
TIMES

Contents

The author modified the names of people and places in this autobiography. This change helps keep their identities safe and ensures anonymity.

God wants your attention.
There is something He wants you to do.

The Backstory

God Causes Awareness

God's existence was perceivable for the first time when I was almost five years old. The Holy Spirit of God affected me in a roundabout way.

A stranger knocked on the door of my family's home one rainy night. I didn't comprehend the purpose and importance of his visit, but later found out he was a member of a nearby church. He wanted to share the story of God's Son, Jesus the Christ, with anyone who would listen.

Mom and Dad extended a warm invitation for him to enter our home to escape the rain. They sat on the couch, listening to the man talk about Holy God. They had heard the story of Jesus many times before, but they listened patiently. Dad was aware of Jesus because of his mom. He had a small New Testament Bible tucked away with his keepsakes. His mom gave it to him before she passed away from cancer when he was young.

The stranger said that Lord God made a perfect world at first. But then, Satan came to earth. He had been cast out of heaven due to his pride and rebellion against God. The evil one approached the first female and spoke with deception. Satan insinuated God was a liar and enticed her to sin against God by being disobedient. Then she tempted her mate to disobey God, too.

Once the people, Adam and Eve, disobeyed, everything changed. In essence, the first couple rejected God and made Satan their ruler. The world was no longer perfect, but it bore curses. The visitor told my parents that from then on, people have been born sinners. The ruler of this world, Satan, has trapped us. His goal is to kill, steal, and destroy God's creation, knowing God loves the world. He tries to take God's place of glory and honor, but he never will. He is a creature, and God is the Creator.

The first couple broke mankind's relationship with God. They became separated from Him because the Lord God is holy and does not allow sin in His presence. God says the penalty for sin is death. Still, God loved mankind and wanted to rescue them from the devil and their awful sin predicament.

God knew, before the creation of the world, that mankind would not be loyal to Him, but He had a plan to deal with evil. Then, when Adam and Eve sinned, God acted right away. He put His plan in motion to save believers from their sins.

"For the wages of sin is death. But the gift of God is eternal life through Christ Jesus our Lord" (Romans 6:23). *"All these new things are from God who brought us back to Himself through what Christ Jesus did. And God has given us the privilege of urging everyone to come into His favor and be reconciled to Him. For God was in Christ, restoring the world to Himself, no longer counting men's sins against them but blotting them out. This is the wonderful message He has given us to tell others."* (2 Corinthians 5:18-19).

Christ Jesus is Father God's only way to restore people to a right relationship with Him. He helps repentant people overcome sin, one step at a time, with the Holy Spirit's strength. (Romans 8)

God's Son, Jesus, the only sinless person who has ever lived in the world, paid your penalty for your sin by dying for you. Then He rose back to life by God's power. Jesus heals the brokenhearted. He proclaims freedom to captives and comforts those who mourn. He also seeks to save the downtrodden, the blind, and the sinner. Jesus, the Messiah, came to save every sinner who will believe, repent, and trust Him.

Both of my parents had heard the Bible story before, and neither had believed before that night. But something stirred in my dad's heart and mind as the visitor spoke. It was the Holy Spirit working. Dad repented of his sins and dedicated his life to the Lord that October night in 1960.

Mom shares in her Christian testimony that she went along with what Dad wanted to do that night. She went through the motions of accepting Christ Jesus with Dad. But she did not see how serious sin is and didn't repent or believe until 30 years later. She didn't understand why obeying God's Word was important. So, during those 30 years of pretense, Mom believed her desires were more important than God's desires. She was unable to think and act like a new creation by following Christ because she was not a new creation.

The stranger's loving sacrifice and strong faith blessed our family. It's impressive that he came to our home during a rainstorm. Most people wouldn't make that effort. Don't most people use the rain as an excuse to keep from sharing God's life-changing news with others? I'm thankful the Lord God was interacting with my family that night, even though we did not perceive it at the time.

We started going to the visitor's church right away and became members. Mom loved going to church and joining in the social events. She even became the church pianist and special singer. Her "good works" made her feel important in the sight of others.

On the other hand, Dad experienced a distinct change. His 24/7 Christ-following behavior indicated he had real love for the Lord. He prayed and studied the Bible often, then put what he learned from the Bible into action. In other words, he walked his talk. Dad also became involved in various loving outreach ministries. His behavior showed that he was much more than a "go-to-church-on-Sunday" Christian.

I suspect Dad's new outlook bothered Mom a lot. He became a different person with priorities that didn't match hers. He had a heavenly view, while my mom continued to focus on her wants and earthly matters. This divide very likely contributed to our family's breakdown a few years later.

Missing the Mark

At eight years old, I saw our artist-pastor make a beautiful drawing during a church service. He used colored chalk on big pastel paper that was propped on a giant easel.

The image depicted people walking on a giant bridge that spanned over a raging gulf of fire. The bridge was a cross that lay across the page. The cross connected the mountaintop on the left to a safe, beautiful place on the right side of the page—heaven. Some people were falling from the cross/bridge into hell's fire below. I loved this art and the symbolism. The message impressed me, and I decided that's where I wanted to be! I wanted to go to heaven after I died. But I did not understand that repentance of sin is vital to reaching the blissful goal.

On occasion, I saw tears in the eyes of people when they went to the front of the sanctuary at the end of some services. I thought crying might be an important thing for me to do. So I pinched my arm hard a few times to produce some tears. Then, I went to the front of the church to receive Jesus.

Everyone in the church, including my mom and my very joyful dad, assumed I had become a Christian that night. But Lord God saw me and knew I didn't understand what sin had to do with anything. I didn't repent of any sins but only wished to be in that beautiful place called heaven--like a lot of other people.

So, Lord God didn't save me at that point, which was later proven by the direction I took in life.

Division, Loss, and Secrets

In 1963, George Hefel came to visit the church where we had become members three years earlier. Mr. Hefel's parents joined that church long before my family did. They were eager to introduce their son to all their friends there. My parents stepped forward to greet the new visitor. Mom reached out to shake the visitor's hand. The moment their fingers touched, she "knew" they were soul mates, she later admitted. Mr. Hefel soon joined the church.

It doesn't take much imagination to figure out what happened after that. Mom had "fallen in love" with the other man, then divorced Dad to live her dream life.

That's when my siblings and I began to learn about multifaceted betrayal. To an outside observer, Mom and her family appeared ethical and moral. It was very important to her that she be well thought of by others outside her home. But she excelled at manipulation, deception, and secret-keeping. She also used her parental authority to silence and control her three children. Chase, Ria, and I became like puppets with no voices of our own. I'd like to note that I'm sure God accomplished His purposes despite Mom's sins and refusal to follow Christ. My upbringing strongly influenced the path of my life and has played a significant part in God's plan. I understand, and I forgave her long ago.

I want to share a strange experience before we jump ahead almost 15 years to avoid my troubled past. Reflecting on the way that later events worked out, the following oddity may be an experience worth noting. I don't want to ignore it—in case.

In my junior year of high school, I painted a symbolic self-portrait. The artwork medium was bright watercolor on canvas board. Then, I gave it to my best friend, Renee, as a going-away gift. The view showed a cross-section of my profile. Inside my skull, instead of a brain, there was a human embryo the size of a brain. I tilted my head up, as if gazing skyward. Shadows covered my eyes, while a strong breeze tousled my hair.

Renee lived with her dad. He liked me a lot and was very friendly when I came to visit her. She showed him my painting, and he became very enthused! He loved it and said he must show it to a certain woman who hosted a séance meeting that he attended each week. He wanted the woman's interpretation. I thought I knew the meaning of my own painting, of course, but he believed there was another, deeper meaning.

A week or so later, her dad stopped being friendly; instead, he was sullen and didn't speak to me—not even "hi." But I noticed he watched, seeming to study me as I moved around in his house while visiting my friend. I've always wondered why he changed his attitude towards me in such a sudden manner.

I asked Renee if her dad took my painting to his woman friend like he had planned. She said he did, but he didn't want to talk about it. We wondered about the mysterious matter.

I wonder if God warned the séance medium and Renee's dad to stay away from me because I was one predestined to be reborn. I think He was protecting me. *"In love He predestined us for adoption to Himself as sons through Jesus Christ... according to the purpose of Him who works all things according to the counsel of His will..."* Ephesians 1:5, 11

Perceptions Begin
and Build

Lord God Comforts

I sat alone in front of a fireplace one specific night at age 25, tears streaming down my face. The love of my life, Charles, not only rejected me after I became pregnant but also accused me of being a liar and a cheat.

What made it worse was that my sister, Ria, had invited me on a blind date to meet him a couple of years earlier. She told me after we broke up that she had known all along that Charles was a drug addict. He and her husband, Johnny, took heroin together all the time, and she didn't mind at all! I had quit all drug activity five years earlier after a friend was murdered in my home. So, Charles hid his addiction from me. I never knew anyone who took heroin, so I didn't notice what I should have seen.

I feared my baby's health might suffer due to my ignorance and foolishness. I wondered if life could get any worse.

After a while of struggling with my grief, I suddenly felt I was not alone in the living room. It seemed that something was at the fireplace hearth in front of me, but I could not see a form. I turned my attention to the hearth, thinking, "What is that?" I squinted my eyes to try to focus while staring across the dimly lit room, and my tears gradually slowed.

Then a commanding thought came to my mind; the thought was something like, "Stop crying. This will be a blessing to many people" or "This one will be a blessing to many people." I don't remember the *exact* words anymore. But the notion was factual, devoid of feeling.

In amazement, I did stop crying. I wasn't a Christian at that time, but I did believe that God created this world and He makes people. I realized in that exact moment that God caused the conception of this baby. I flashed back in my mind to the steps that led to my pregnancy.

1). I didn't notice until the end of the day on Friday that my birth control pills had gone missing.

2). I searched everywhere I thought the pills could be. Then, I phoned my doctor's office to ask for an emergency prescription to keep my weekend pill schedule.

3). A male voice told me in a rough tone that I was irresponsible and that no one would grant a prescription so late in the day.

4). Then, I told myself, "I'll abstain on our next date." But I later changed my mind and gave in. I figured the odds of becoming pregnant were way too high to be concerned.

5). A couple of days later, I found my birth control pill container at the bottom of my four-year-old son Mike's toy box. I understood how he would view it as a toy. He must have climbed up on the bathroom sink to get it. I felt relieved when I found it and thought I was in the clear.

While sitting across from the fireplace, I suddenly saw purpose in this awful but miraculous situation. I felt comforted, believing God had a plan that included me.

Soon thereafter, I told Mom and my stepfather about my pregnancy. It was difficult. They expressed a strong desire for me to have an abortion and attempted to persuade me. But they couldn't talk me into it.

After becoming a Christian years later, I read Genesis 21. It tells how the angel of the Lord spoke to Hagar, a non-believer. The angel comforted her about her son, Ishmael. From my perspective, the Lord comforted me in a similar way that sorrowful night at the fireplace.

The Lord God spoke through His prophet in Ezekiel 34:16, saying, *"I will search for the lost and bring back the strays. I will bind up the injured and strengthen the weak..."* Jesus said in John 10:10, *"The thief comes only to steal, kill, and destroy. I have come that they may have life and have it to the full."*

Looking back, I see how God was preparing and guiding me. He revealed Himself slowly throughout my life, leading me to salvation years later.

God enables

I found out I was pregnant in November 1981. This was right before I applied for my second drafting job. My pregnancy was not yet observable, so I kept the fact a secret from the company during the application and interview process.

A few days later, they told me I was hired. I suddenly felt awful about not informing them of my pregnancy.

On my first day, I went straight to the president of the company and told him, "I'm sorry I kept this from you, but I'm pregnant. I will need to take off from work for at least six weeks after the baby is born. So, I'll understand if you change your mind about hiring me. I was deceitful and should not have put you in this position. I'm sorry."

The president said he appreciated my candor and asked me to wait in the lobby for a while. He talked with the engineer as well as the man who would be my manager about the situation. They decided to put me to a test.

The manager called me to his office and told me of their decision. He said they would be glad to hire me if I met certain conditions. I must study the blueprints of their unique building system by myself. Then, within five days, I must design a commercial building with the specific dimensions and other building requirements that were needed. The set of drawings would consist of a plot plan, a floor plan, and three elevations. If I succeeded, I could keep the job. If I failed to understand the system and/or could not finish the plans within five days, they would have to let me go.

I didn't know Lord God back then, but I do know and was very aware at the time that He helped me to understand. At first, the blueprints on the drafting board looked like a puddle of mud. But as I stared longer, the murkiness faded. Soon, I could see and understand everything clearly! I completed the task before the deadline. They were thrilled, and so was I. My job as a full-time drafts-person was secure.

I sometimes drew for the architectural department, and sometimes for the engineering department. It was enjoyable working with such a smart and fun mix of multicultural individuals. Being employed there was such a joy, and my income was so much more than I thought I'd ever earn.

This experience showed me that God is very good and cares for all people. *"For He makes His sun to shine on bad and good people alike and gives rain to those who do good and to those who do evil."* (Matthew 5:45) The Bible also says the Lord gives people skill to do all kinds of work. I was very appreciative of His help and knew I could not have done the work without Him. Matter of a fact, throughout my employment with this wonderful company, I often told Him, "Thank you, God!" I meant it with all sincerity, too.

This is another example of how God has been guiding and showing Himself to me over the years. He worked slowly, leading me to salvation.

God Directs

I had a nervous breakdown in 1984 after experiencing another love-interest failure. I wondered if there was any good reason to continue living. I was blind to everything good and positive during that time, for I focused on what I couldn't have instead of what I did have.

Life seemed to be nothing but a long series of heartbreaks and tragedies. I was sorry my sons had to live in such a terrible world. Their futures seemed as bleak as my own, and I grieved to imagine their future sorrows.

My viewpoint caused my mom and stepfather to worry about my sons, ages six and almost two. So, I let them take my boys to live in a small country town—supposedly with temporary custody.

I was able to realize that my thinking wasn't healthy. I knew I had to take steps to improve my thought life. So, after my boys left, I started treatment with a psychologist and kept working at my drafting job. Within six months, my mental health had improved a lot.

I notified my mom that I was ready for my sons to return to me, but Mom and my stepfather refused to let them come home. They said if I wanted my sons, I'd need to move my mobile home onto their property. Their excuse was that Richmond had become too dangerous for children. What could I say to that since kidnappings were on the rise? So, I quit my wonderful job and moved to that rural area to be near my sons.

One job didn't provide the income I needed, so I took a full-time job along with one and two part-time jobs (off and on) to cover my bills. My primary employer was the local newspaper. I formed a good friendship with a coworker, Jim, the newspaper journalist. After the workday, we met often at a local bar. I started drinking whiskey and Coke on a regular basis. Before long, drinking became a crutch I felt I needed. I spent too little time with my sons except on weekends.

Something strange began happening during the nights in September 1989. Without thinking about it, I often found myself looking up from the ground in an instant. My focus went straight to a specific set of stars. This happened night after night at least once or more times each night. I never had to search for that set; they were always right there before my eyes, no matter the time of night. No matter where I was standing or what I was doing, I looked up without thinking and immediately faced the set.

It was so eerie! I became very alarmed and actually

screamed one time when it happened while I was speaking to a friend. Of course, I wondered, "Why is my focus always going to that set of stars? What constellation is that?" During my research, I found that it was the constellation of Orion that drew my attention.

As soon as I read the constellation's name, I remembered God. He helped me solve problems in my drafting work in Richmond. The thought sprang to my mind that God was proving He could grab my attention and put my focus on whatever He chooses! What an astonishing revelation!

Psalm 135:6 says, *"Whatever the Lord pleases, He does, in heaven and on earth, in the seas and all deeps."* Yes, I'm here to testify that God is sovereign. He has complete control over everything. He does whatever He likes in order to achieve His will and purposes. He knows how to let people exercise their will—good or bad—while He does His own will. That's a mind-boggling concept that's too hard for a human to grasp!

I discovered a few months later that God's Word notes the constellation of Orion—twice in the Book of Job and once in the Book of Amos. These verses show God's total control over the heavens. They highlight His authority, greatness, and the vastness of creation.

Even when I was unaware of His notice and living in sin, God provided subtle guidance. He prepared and revealed Himself to me bit by bit, leading me to salvation soon after.

God Requires Reverence

Not long after the Orion object lesson taught me that God can direct a person's focus, the words, "Stop drinking" came to mind. It happened several times within two or three weeks. I felt this thought wasn't mine because I truly enjoyed drinking for many reasons. I assumed God was giving me a command.

Not wanting to be disrespectful, I told Him out loud that I would consider His command. But I planned in my heart to keep drinking. I enjoyed the taste of whiskey and Coke and the feelings it gave me. I figured I would at least tell Him I'd think about it out of respect for His office as Creator.

A few days later, the thought "Stop drinking" popped into my mind again. I was at home, wide awake, enjoying the peace.

It was Friday, October 13, 1989. The words "Stop drinking" came to mind again. I valued God's concern for my well-being, but I felt it was unwarranted. So, I spoke up aloud to reassure Him. "Okay, I've thought about it. I want You to know that drinking helps me to relax. It helps me get over my reclusive nature and be less inhibited. Also, it helps me think; I feel a little smarter after a few drinks. Besides all else, I get along better with people; alcohol makes me more loving and sociable." I shared these reasons for staying in my relationship with alcohol. Then I told God, "I know You want me to stop, but I'm not gonna quit drinking." Thanks anyway for Your concern."

I remained quiet for a moment. I felt relaxed and satisfied with my tranquil country life. But about a minute after my speech, I felt something tickle under my nose—right above my upper lip. I touched that area with my fingers out of curiosity. Blood from my nose caused the tickle.

How astonishing! Never in my life had I experienced a nosebleed—much less a nosebleed that seemed to occur for no reason at all! I immediately concluded that God must have 'popped' me (so to speak) for refusing to obey Him. Then I got angry to think He could be so pushy, but at the same time, the fear of God shook me for the first time in my life.

My reaction was to jump up and look at my face in the bathroom mirror. I stood there in total amazement in front of the mirror and watched the line of blood trickle down from my nose. Still scared but angry, I turned and stomped to the toilet. I grabbed some toilet paper to wipe away the blood. As I stomped, I exclaimed out loud and loudly, "OKAY! If You're going to be THAT way about it, I'll QUIT!"

Turning back to the mirror to clean up my face, I noticed the blood flow was stopping. It was shocking to see my nose heal so quickly after I told God that I would quit drinking. I began trembling—literally—with fear. My heart was pounding in my neck, and great weakness overtook my body. Wide-eyed and breathless, I sat down on the toilet lid in shock. I trembled, replaying the last few minutes over and over. My mind was so blown!

I began to experience real reverence for God. He was obviously the Boss of everything! I kept my word to God and never drank again. Each time I've been tempted to take another drink, I remember God then choose obedience.

I didn't become a Christian during this experience, so I wasn't saved. But the Lord was drawing me in and getting me ready for salvation shortly after.

Looking back, I realize that a key part of saving faith was missing from my life. That part was godly fear, and I had not understood it until that day. *"The fear of the LORD is the beginning of wisdom, and the knowledge of the Holy One is understanding"* (Proverbs 9:10). This is yet another important example of God preparing and revealing Himself to me bit by bit. He was leading me to salvation.

The Ultimate Reality

Lord God causes Rebirth

On December 11, 1989, the Holy Spirit prompted me to buy a Bible. I went to a Christian bookstore at a local mall and browsed the wide selection of Bibles. After a while of searching, I picked the "just-right one" from the many options.

I took my new NKJV Bible home. I sat cross-legged on my bed and raised the Book. I asked God out loud to teach me from it. My eyes were wide open while I spoke to Him as if He were a human standing and listening at the foot of my bed. I told Him I didn't want to learn from preachers. The arguing among denominations bothered me a lot. I also refused to read the study notes. Whoever wrote them might not have understood. I believed God was the only One who could teach me truth.

I started reading my new Bible every day, beginning with Genesis 1:1. I took my time with each word to grasp as much meaning as I could. The only study tool I used, but very rarely, was Strong's Concordance to determine definitions. I felt a strong pull to Scripture, much like a magnet to steel. I read His Holy Word daily whenever I could. It was surprising how the stories drew me in.

The night of January 2, 1990, I worked very late to meet the newspaper deadline. The newspaper publisher allowed me sleep in his office on deadline nights. I spread a pallet of blankets on the floor and picked up my Bible, continuing from where I had stopped the day before. Then I read and stopped reading at the end of Genesis chapter 49 that night.

I lay on the pallet in the dark, thinking about what I had read. Then, God removed the scales from my eyes. I finally saw my awful wretchedness in contrast to His magnificent glory! I cried as I repented of my sins. I especially mourned about the lies I told a friend about God's character and salvation. I didn't know I had lied to my friend. I spoke out of ignorance. Still, I was guilty of lying since my words weren't God's truth.

I cried myself to sleep—hating my sinful predicament.

After I fell asleep, and in the wee hours of January 3, 1990, I dreamed. Waves of water washed over me, flowing from head to toe, then toe to head, in a continuous and slow rhythm. During this time, I felt amazing joy. I kept saying a strange word over and over. It was from another language.

I moved my arms as if to hug and hold onto the Someone there with me and begged Him not to leave me. Then I heard Him speak a sentence that I cannot bring myself to share but will remember it to my dying day! His words surprised me so much that I awoke immediately.

I lay there in complete astonishment and didn't want to move even a little finger. The experience was amazing and mind-blowing. I wanted to hold onto that memory without the distraction of movement.

As I lay on the pallet, I thought about the foreign word that I spoke over and over during the dream. When my curiosity got the best of me, I finally made myself move to do research on the mysterious word. I could remember it with only a faint clarity. But I knew I would recognize it after searching my copy of Strong's Concordance. It lay on the floor, within arm's reach.

The miracle I found was shocking: I was saying the Hebrew word "Shiloh." This means "Messiah" and appears in Genesis 49:10. I had read that Scripture before sleeping! When first reading that verse, I did not comprehend the meaning of Shiloh. I praise God for bringing Himself to my attention and ensuring that the Word did not slip by me!

I later discovered in the Bible that the Lord baptized me with the Holy Spirit. I read, *"He (meaning Messiah Jesus) will baptize you with the Holy Spirit and fire,"* in Matthew 3:11. The Messiah brings spiritual transformation through the Holy Spirit and purifies through fire. I actually FELT brand new and clean! I later read 2 Corinthians 5:17: *"If anyone is in Christ, he is a new creature. Old things have passed away; all things are new."*

Many Bible verses show that Jesus talks to believers. A key verse is John 10:27-28: *"My sheep hear My voice, and I know them, and they follow Me."* How can anyone resist a God who speaks through His written Word, keeps promises, has given His life to redeem sinners, then empowers His followers to take part in the abundance of all that He offers?

So many things written in the Bible were happening to me before I learned about them! Magnificent are the ways of the majestic Lord God and how He works with great understanding!

Lord God desires obedience

The Lord blessed me right away with enough wisdom to understand some of what pleases Him and what doesn't. I later found support for this statement in Proverbs 2:6. It says, *"For the Lord gives wisdom; from His mouth come knowledge and understanding."* As soon as I got home from the newspaper office, right after the Lord saved me, I threw away all my provocative clothes. I also trashed makeup and other beauty items that I had used to attract the attention of men.

Lord God made it clear to me that He hates fornication. So right away, I stopped dating the man I cared about after explaining to him my desire to do the will of the Lord. He didn't get it, but that's okay. It wasn't his time. I chose to stay celibate to please the magnificent Creator and lover of all things good. I was starving for God and wanted only Him.

My soul burst with joy when I read King David's praise:

"As a deer pants for the water brooks, so pants my soul for You, O God!" Psalm 42:1. King David was indicating his desperate yearning for God's presence, and I could identify--even though the reasons for our desperation were a bit different.

Lord God gives Witness To His Glory

A few months after my salvation, I was still reading the Bible daily. I started writing a weekly devotional article for the newspaper. After a while, I titled it *"Revelation of the Mystery."* I got no complaints from the public. Christians were encouraging and appreciated me hammering on the subjects of salvation and doing the will of the Lord. The publisher allowed me to print a weekly Bible reading schedule, too.

I began buying Bibles by the case. I gave a Bible to everyone I met who didn't have one and told them about the Lord. I read later that Mark 16:15 instructs Christians to *"Go into all the world and preach the gospel to all creation."*

Eight months after my rebirth, I was continuing to read the Word each day. That's about the time I finally turned on the radio and found a worshipful Christian station--KHCB FM. I heard a wonderful teacher named Dr. John MacArthur Jr. I could hear the Lord's voice, so to speak, when he preached. So I began listening to him regularly with lots of joy. He believed the scriptures like me! Then, God prompted me to start visiting my brothers and sisters in Christ at different churches around town. I saw the Lord work mightily as I looked for a church home.

One of the people I witnessed to, Mark, was a fellow who drank in the same bar that I used to frequent. He admitted that he was aware I "got religion" and didn't believe I was going to stop drinking. He said he watched to see if I'd return to the bar. He expressed amazement that I was still on this new path to a different life. He asked how I was able to stop drinking.

I told Mark that Lord God rescued me from the path leading to destruction. I gave him a Bible and told him how the Lord Jesus saves us from having to pay the penalty for our own sins.

A month or so later, Mark contacted me. He was so excited and eager to tell me that he had been reading the Bible. The Lord had saved him, too, and he found a church home! He thanked me over and over for sharing the good news with him! Like me, he became a zealous witness to God's glory.

1 Peter 1:8-9 describes the feelings of a believer in Christ: *"Though you have not seen Him, you love Him. Though you do not now see Him, you believe in Him and rejoice with joy that is inexpressible and filled with glory, obtaining the outcome of your faith, the salvation of your souls."*

Several months later, Mark died and entered into the presence of the Lord. 2 Corinthians 5:8 lets us know a couple of things -- when we are away from the body, we are in the presence of the Lord. Death is not something believers fear, but rather than staying in our bodies, we prefer to be with the Lord. I praise God that Mark chose life before passing into eternity.

Lord God Heals

Another glorious miracle happened one day at Carter's Grocery Store. It was part of my job to create an advertisement, a 4-page color tabloid, for that supermarket each week. Customers received the tab by mail, and stores also distributed it.

I was a smidgen late for my appointment with Mr. Carter. I rushed down the aisles toward his office, which was upstairs at the back of the store. As I moved through the produce section, I saw an elderly man shuffling down the aisle. I slowed down a bit as I passed him and said as

I went by, "Hi there, how are you doing?" I had already passed by him at least four or five feet when I heard him say behind me, "I'm not doing very well at all." I stopped immediately and turned back to ask him, "What's wrong?" I felt alarmed to see a cloud-like white layer of something covering his eyeballs. I don't recall ever seeing eyes like that. He told me in a sad and quiet voice that his wife had died not long ago, and he was having trouble with his sight.

I said, "I'm so sorry to hear about that. I will pray for you. What's your name?" He told me his name was Moses and that his son's church had been praying for him for several months. I told him as I started to dash away, "I'll pray for you, too."

Then the Lord told me to pray for Moses right then and there in the produce department. James 5:15 is one of several scriptures that say the prayer of faith will save the one who is sick. I thought to the Lord as I hurried down the aisle, "I'm late for my appointment and need to go," then kept up the speed walk. The closer I got to the back of the store, the heavier my conviction felt. Each step up the stairs to Mr. Carter's office added to the weight like pounds pressing down on me.

I grieved that I had not obeyed the Lord. When I reached Mr. Carter's office, I was lost in thoughts of Moses. I struggled to focus on what Mr. Carter was saying about the ad. I tried to locate Moses through the long line of windows overlooking the store as Mr. Carter talked to me. I finally got everything in writing that he wanted in his ad for the coming week. I dashed back down the stairs and ran from aisle to aisle across the whole store looking for Moses and didn't find him.

I jogged to the front of the store and asked a worker if he knew the elderly man named Moses. He said yes and that he had left the store a little while ago. I asked him if he happened to know where Moses lives. He knew the way and gave me directions. I don't think it was more than a couple of miles away; it was pretty easy to find. He lived in a very poor area of town. Moses lived in a leaning, tiny, and ragged-looking shack. An old and torn-up bench seat taken out of a vehicle was on the dirt near the front door. I stepped onto the unleveled wooden porch and knocked.

Moses came to the door. I explained that the Lord had been pressing me hard to pray for him in person, so I asked him if he'd mind. He smiled and invited me in. We sat on a nearby dilapidated old couch where I grabbed his thin hand and began praying like the Lord wanted me to. After I finished, he smiled and seemed very appreciative. Moses said, "I KNOW the Lord heard that prayer."

He shared that his son is a leader in the Jehovah's Witnesses Kingdom Hall. He also noted that the group had been praying several months for him. I didn't want to challenge Moses about his son's false beliefs. I told him I have discovered that God's Word fits well with Protestant theology. However, many followers of Christ could have stronger faith—myself included sometimes. We talked a little while longer, and I left.

I saw Moses only one more time in my life, and it was a couple of weeks later. I saw him walk up to the front doors of Carter's grocery store. I was close behind in the parking lot. I was there to do my weekly advertising duty for Mr. Carter. When I saw the back of him, I called out, "Hey, is that you, Moses?" He turned to look at me. It was shocking how fast the Lord healed Moses's eyes!

I said something like, "Wow, Moses! Did you have surgery on your eyes? They look so good!" He seemed surprised that I would say such a thing, and I was ashamed to have said it. He shook his head and said with a big smile that it was God who healed him. He said he didn't have surgery, but his vision was a lot better. Praise the Lord!

Scripture is replete with instances of Jesus' healing power. Any of the gospels—Matthew, Mark, Luke or John—bear witness to Christ's power. The keys to witnessing or perceiving God's power are faith, obedience to His written Word, and trust.

Grateful for Blessings

We shouldn't serve the Lord for what we can gain materially. He is the Most High and Supreme God who deserves all the glory we can express to Him. Our love from the heart and service to Him and others is what He wants. He's not a genie, and He's not going to behave like one in order to provide your selfish heart's desires.

Due to His mercy and compassion, God blesses both believers and unbelievers. These blessings include health, wealth, and more. But He will act according to His plans and purposes. Some people believe they are entitled or deserve to have their wishes granted. Others think their own actions lead to their successes. James 1:17 says, *"Every good and perfect gift is from above, coming down from the Father of the heavenly lights."*

In 1991, I wanted to own a house but wasn't looking for one yet. During that time, I explored different denominations in the area to find a church home. Then, a Christian couple from a nearby Methodist church came to me.

The Christian gentleman mentioned that he heard I wanted a house in town. Mr. Vin said he knew I hoped my sons would leave their grandparents' house and live with me. He said he knew of a house for sale. He asked me to go look at it and let him know what I thought. I found it was in walking distance to the junior and senior high schools and was in very good condition. I loved it!

This kind Christian couple bought the house for me. Then, they let me buy it back for only $200 a month over ten years! But after eight years, he told me I could stop making payments. Mr. Vin paid my debt and presented me with the house deed!

After moving into the house in 1991, a small bush in front grew quickly. It soon reached over 6 feet tall and bloomed lots of lovely small red flowers. That ornamental plant was such a lovely decoration for my front yard. I had never seen one like it.

One day, my 97-year-old neighbor, Samuel, came by. He loved Christ and wanted to introduce himself. He also brought food as a kind gesture. He said he had lived next door for years. He had never seen the plant grow so high and flowers bloom so abundantly before I moved in.

It touched my heart to know the Lord was giving me fresh and beautiful flowers! The first verses of Deuteronomy 11 highlight blessings for those who love and serve Him.

One blessing is to have land that *"drinks water by the rain from heaven, a land cared for by the LORD your God. The eyes of the LORD your God are always on it."* You might think that you can hardly count these flowers as a blessing. But I see them as a gift showing God's loving kindness. He likes people to appreciate Him. *"O give thanks to the Lord for He is good, for His steadfast love endures forever."* I love how He loves me.

My dear elderly neighbor passed away inside his home in 1992. A family member of his came to my home later to break the news about Samuel. He told me that relatives gathered for a final get-together because he was close to passing away. As Samuel lay on his bed, he told his family he could see Jesus; He was there in the room.

Minutes later, he left his bed and this world to be with the Lord. Isaiah 57:2 builds on verse 1, discussing the righteous. It says, *"He shall enter into peace; they shall rest in their beds, each one walking in his uprightness."* This verse shows that peace and rest come after death for those who follow the Triune God.

Lord God Chastises the Disobedient With Consequences

I visited several church groups for a while as I searched for a church home. I started attending services often at a Baptist church located outside of town. I knew that I needed to undergo baptism in water to fulfill God's desire for believers. Pastor Den baptized me on February 17, 1991. The baptistery was full of murky water. I felt thrilled to see the dark water. I liked pretending I was being baptized in the Jordan River! My baptism put me on the membership roll of that small country church.

Over the course of time, I began hearing messages from the pulpit that alarmed me. Some messages rang in my soul like a sour note. I wasn't hearing Jesus' voice—so to speak. It wasn't God's truth. I wondered what to do— look for another church home?

I stayed a while longer and waited for the Lord's prompting. Not long after a church service, I stood outside with others. The pastor and the head deacon came over and took me aside for a private talk. The head deacon handed a paperback book to me. It described the author's method for delivering people from demons. The pastor asked me to read it. He also wanted me to pray about joining their new demon deliverance ministry.

I was pretty surprised since I had not heard him preach on this subject. After a quick read of the book the next week, I noticed something that concerned me. It seemed to focus too much on demonic activity and not enough on the power of Jesus. I'm not saying the Lord does not call and use chosen believers to deliver people from demons. Frankly, I believe there are Christians gifted and called to this particular ministry. But I do not believe the average Christian has the faith to command demons with effect like that particular book seemed to indicate. If someone calls himself a Christian and tries to cast out demons but has not been gifted for the task, and especially if he does not follow the Lord in obedience and holiness, I'd say that person would likely be headed for a LOT of demonic troubles.

I viewed the off-kilter focus of that particular book as dangerous and declined the pastor's and head deacon's offer to join them. I figured this was my cue to start looking for another church home. The Lord allowed them to walk that path for some reason, but that wasn't the direction the Lord God wanted me to take.

At that same time, organizers scheduled a so-called revival in a nearby city. The pastor encouraged church members to attend. He said other church groups would be there for a revival and healing service. I was skeptical, but attended the huge event anyway out of curiosity.

Hundreds of people were there. A few days prior, I read a certain passage from the Old Testament. I felt that God helped me grasp its meaning to at least a small degree. The preacher at the revival read the same passage. I felt astonished and disgusted at the way he twisted the meaning! When I heard his shocking and incorrect view, the Lord told me to leave the service right away. But I disobeyed the Lord, saying to Him, "I want to see what will happen during their healing service." The Lord was bearing down on me to go. I stayed, knowing the Holy Spirit was pressing, pressing, pressing me hard to leave. I watched six or eight other people get up from their seats and leave the auditorium at that time. Those people were faithful Christians who chose to be obedient to the Triune God.

At the end of the false message, the person at the podium invited people to come to the front who needed healing. I sat at the back of the auditorium and did not move. I sat and watched and no longer felt the Lord prompting me to leave. They turned the lights down low.

A few minutes after the speaker's invitation, a young woman came and invited me to the front. I told her I didn't want to go. She actually took hold of my arm and pulled me from my seat. I didn't want to make a scene, so I stayed quiet. I pulled back while she used her strength to pull me forward.

I noticed that both my pastor and his wife were lying down on the raised stage. They lay on the floor, facing up, in a deep sleep. They believed they were doing right by the Lord and wanted to be there on the floor for some very strange reason. It seemed I was in the Twilight Zone!

The strong woman grabbed my arm and pulled me to the main speaker. He was a tall man who studied me for a few seconds without smiling. Then he asked in a loud, commanding, and accusing tone of voice, "What is THAT around your neck?" I wore a thin chain with a small pendant by James Avery. It featured the Alpha and Omega in gold from the Greek alphabet. The two characters were intertwined with artistic skill. I answered him, "It's the Alpha and Omega, representing Jesus." The man yelled at me with a tone of anger, "YOU PRACTICE WITCHCRAFT!" Then he pursed his lips and blew his breath hard towards my face. All at once, an unseen force hit me hard and knocked me almost off my feet. I caught my balance as my hand hit the floor, then stood and ran out of that place in great fear.

I am sure the impostor recognized me as the enemy, and his accusation was close to truth. But the actual truth was that I had rebelled against the Lord God. *"Rebellion is as the sin of witchcraft"* (1 Samuel 15:23). That man's spiritual influencer knew I followed the Lord. He also realized I was disobeying Him by being there. I'm confident.

I felt as if I had been spiritually raped. The Lord was not to blame. It was my fault for disobeying. But something in me changed immediately. One indication that something was different is that instead of wearing the humbling head covering that I always wore when speaking to the Lord since the day He saved me, inhibition and fear was my covering. I suspect the same ungodly spirits also cover most American Christians for we can certainly be influenced. We can get rid of that awful and restrictive covering, though, by continually pressing towards obedience to the written Word and holiness—every day.

For years, I've wondered what exactly happened that day. Why did my worship change almost in the blink of an eye? What, besides pride and rebellion, was the problem?

The answer may have dawned on me today while considering this true story. The night of the false revival, I related to the Lord like a lot of women relate to their human husbands. When the Lord told me to leave the auditorium, I didn't see myself as disobeying. I imagined interacting with a familiar man, a husband, who loves me. This loving person would tolerate my occasional stubbornness. He would give in to my wishes because of his love. I was not relating to the Lord God as the Most High and Sovereign Creator of all. My incorrect view of God harmed my relationship with Him and my worship. Pride, rebellion, and presumption were my problems.

I repent and pray to always revere Him in ways that honor Him as the majestic Triune God that He is. May I never again relate to Him as if He were a mere dependent and/or compromising human.

After that awful night, I couldn't bring myself to worship with others for several weeks. The Lord allowed some healing time, then prompted me to find a new church group when I read Hebrews. The author wrote, *"And let us consider how to stir up one another to love and good works, not neglecting to meet together, as is the habit of some, but encouraging one another, and all the more as you see the Day drawing near."*

God Uses Our Evil Choices
to Accomplish His Purposes

My sons decided, in time, to come live with me in my new home to be nearer to their friends in town. I didn't care about their motivation because they were older kids by then. Their desires were understandable. I was just glad to have them with me.

In 1993, I began taking my eldest, Mike, to a music store each week. He had guitar lessons taught by a talented musician named Jake. At first, my youngest son, Andy, and I goofed off while waiting for Mike's lessons to end. Before long, my sons and I often stayed afterward and chatted with the teacher.

One day, Jake invited us out to eat—then before I knew it, we all started dating together regularly. The more we dated, the more my sons looked forward to his companionship. They grew to love Jake, who was an over-sized kid himself. He loved doing boy things like making models, talking about cars, and playing rock music. My sons began hinting at marriage, and Jake went right along with their idea. I don't remember him asking me to marry him. I also can't recall any ring presentation. But the three guys agreed that living life together would be wonderful. They looked to me for a "yes" to the idea of marriage.

Jake was a nice guy, very good-looking, talented, and pleasant to get along with. Charismatic. I don't remember any of us ever having a cross word with him. But I had no peace in my heart. I didn't want to marry a man who said he was Christian but loved everything else more than God. He didn't even know what a Scripture reference was. This surprised me because he claimed he had grown up in church. That bothered me a lot since the Lord was my primary thought. I wanted a husband who would be a spiritual leader of the family.

I believed the Lord was telling me not to go through with it. So, I talked to my pastor, Lyle, about my doubts. Pastor Lyle believed that Jake was "a baby Christian" and I shouldn't worry too much about it. He said it would take time for him to grow in the Lord. He pointed out that the marriage would be good for my sons. He encouraged me to go through with it. I did realize and agree that my sons sure did need an involved man.

I went against what I believed the Lord was directing me to do. Like Abraham and Sarah, I chose to do what made human sense. I married Jake on November 25, 1993—Thanksgiving Day. You'll soon know the irony.

About six weeks later, one day during the first week of 1994, Jake didn't come home from work. He vanished. I was confused by his disappearance. We hadn't argued about anything, and everything seemed fine. The boys and I figured he must of had a wreck or encountered foul play.

I learned from his employer at the music store that he didn't show up for work. Also, many guitars, instruments, and other items went missing from the store. We were all very astonished and baffled. It seemed as if I might have married a thief, but how could we know for sure? What if a robber came, took all the music store stuff, then killed Jake and hid his body somewhere? I didn't know what to think. I called hospitals in the area and filed a missing person's report with the police.

Andy grieved intensely and slept on the floor by the front door in tears for several nights. He yearned to be the first person to see Jake return home. As time marched on, Andy seemed to become more troubled. He started turning to his brother and other older guys of poor influence for guidance and approval. After Jake disappeared, Mike changed, too. He went from being a fun-loving comedian to someone arrogant and disrespectful.

I arranged for my sons to get therapy from a Christian counselor on a weekly basis. But Andy refused to speak to the therapist at all, so I didn't force it. Mike seemed to enjoy the therapy visits, so I kept taking him. In time, he admitted he was ready to stop counseling.

After Jake disappeared, I took my sons to a Baptist church east of town. The youth group was active in ways that gave glory to God, and I admired Pastor Bob's ability to preach the Word accurately. I often prayed in tears for a Christian man, or men, in that church group to care for my sons. I was even so bold as to ask a couple of men to spend some time with my boys. And they did, but only a time or two. The Lord didn't prompt anyone in my church group with a desire to reach out to my sons. This led me to wonder if He had other plans for us. I wondered if the Lord was indicating that their step-granddad was the only human father figure they needed. But later, the Lord did move two men from another congregation to show a measure of care toward my sons. The Lord's work was being accomplished but not in a way I hoped or expected. It's okay, though; God's will be done!

In 1994, at age 16, Mike began having torturous pain in his abdomen. He admitted to me and a medical doctor that he had been sneaking and drinking alcohol. The doctor decided the boy had pancreatitis because he drank alcohol. The doctor suggested several treatments over weeks, but nothing helped Mike's health. He got much worse.

My son was close to death when an ambulance took him to a hospital in a nearby city. An emergency room doctor saved his life by quickly discovering the real problem. He said Mike didn't drink enough alcohol to cause pancreatitis. Instead, stones in his pancreas caused his health problems. The stones had been there too long and were causing gangrene. Part of Mike's pancreas had to be removed as soon as possible.

Mike had a lot of poison in his system. This made the operation risky. The doctor couldn't predict the outcome. As I sat in the hospital lobby with family waiting for his surgery to end, I felt profound peace. It was the kind of peace that is beyond understanding. I had complete trust in the Lord and believed Romans 8:28. *"And we know that in all things God works for the good of those who love Him, who have been called according to His purpose."* Admittedly, the good spoken of in that verse can feel terrible in some cases, but there is purpose. We are to be conformed, even in "bad" experiences, to the image of Christ.

My stepfather was very irritated with me because of my peaceful demeanor. He accused me of not caring for my son and surmised that I looked forward to him dying. I tried to explain the peace that the Lord gave me, but he didn't understand. I wasn't offended. He simply couldn't understand Philippians 4:7. *"And the peace of God, which surpasses all understanding, will guard your hearts and minds through Christ Jesus."* The Lord was guarding my heart and mind from fear and worry.

Mike survived the pancreatic surgery, but it caused him to become diabetic. He must have daily insulin shots for life. After being released from the hospital, he stayed with his grandparents for a while. Then he moved back home to live with me and Andy. That was about the time we learned what had happened to Jake.

In early 1995, over a year after Jake vanished, I got a call from the Birmingham Police Department. The officer noticed a missing person's report I had filed soon after Jake's disappearance. After all this time, he was finally arrested. That's when I found out he was a con man, a thief, and he was married multiple times.

His con game was to marry Christian women to gain advantages; and he stole from them and his employers. Jake admitted to me on a jail phone that he decided not to steal from me like he had from other women. He said it was because he cared a lot for my sons. I knew it was true but I was dismayed. How could he leave them like he did? But then again, I know the Bible reveals that the Lord God chased or drove individuals away from His chosen people a number of times for their protection.

Since the day that Jake went missing, I had grieved for my sons. But my grief for my sons was made worse by knowing this entire situation was all my fault. I had gone against the will of the Lord—again! I knew I should not have married Jake. Besides, he was married to someone else in the eyes of the Lord, and I had been unwittingly committing adultery!

My little sister, Ria, spent years incarcerated in jails and prisons before she died. I don't know why I didn't consider getting into that type of ministry before. God's timing must have been the issue. But after my experience with Jake, I began to suspect God was pointing me to jail and prison ministry. Mom then told me that Dad had ministered to incarcerated people when I was a kid. That information motivated me more; I had been a daddy's girl and had missed him since he died in my youth. I liked the idea of following in his footsteps. I sent Bibles and Christian books to the chaplain in Birmingham. I also prayed for Jake and the other inmates to be saved.

This was about the time that Mike did something terrible. But I didn't learn about it until a few weeks later. You will know about it shortly.

For a little while, I stayed in communication with Jake. I had forgiven him for Christ's sake. He couldn't help it. He acted like an unsaved person because he was one. This was clear from his total lack of spiritual fruit. Jesus says we will know others by their fruit. Anyone can say they're a Christian and even read the Bible all the time. But saying "I'm a Christian" only holds true if they are truly born again. They need to be a new creation in Christ (John 3:3, 2 Corinthians 5:17). This means having a heart of flesh, not stone (Ezekiel 36:26). Also, the Bible says a true follower of Christ will follow His commands (John 14:15), most of the time anyway. I thank God for repentance! I need it daily.

I hope I'm not causing genuine Christians to doubt their salvation by making some of those comments, but the Lord does tell us through apostle Paul to examine ourselves. If you are doubting your salvation, I encourage you to read *"The Gospel According to Jesus"* by Dr. John MacArthur Jr. He will help you to know for sure where you stand in God's sight.

Anyway, the day came when a police detective knocked at my door. He told me that authorities suspected my son, Mike, of committing a crime a few weeks earlier. There was an eyewitness. He asked if Mike was there. No, he wasn't; he was with friends. The detective gave me his business card and asked me to call the next time I saw my son.

We later found out that Mike and three of his friends robbed a store in town. My son held the gun and shot toward the storekeeper, shattering a mirror behind the man. Was my son trying to find a way to get into the jail and prison system to meet up with Jake? The idea was far-fetched, but Mike loved his guitar teacher. It makes sense that Jake would somehow be an influence.

At age 17, authorities charged him with aggravated robbery in March 1995. They jailed him. His step-grandfather bailed him out. While he was out on bail, Mike committed two more aggravated robberies with friends. Authorities brought more charges against him, and his step-grandfather bailed him out again.

Mike lived with his grandparents during that time. After many months of arraignments, hearings, and a trial, he was sentenced to prison in August 1996. He was 18 and had recently graduated from an alternative high school.

My life experiences helped to convince me that God was directing me to jail/prison ministry. I joined Prison Fellowship classes, read a lot of literature, and hosted seminars at church. Prison chaplains led the seminars. A group of people from various Christian denominations in my area wanted to rebuild the ruined chapel at a nearby prison. I joined the group. Members selected me to handle the advertising because of my experience with newspapers.

Since that time, the Lord has continued to work in perceivable ways. I'm in the process of continuing to record my stories. If God is willing, they will be published later--after I discover the end of each testimony of God's interactions.

A Bible Synopsis

God is three co-equal and co-eternal persons—the Father, Son, and Holy Spirit. God is holy, pure, righteous, loving, patient, merciful, gracious, and perfect. He hates sin; it provokes Him to wrath. He requires justice.

The Triune God knew the end from the beginning. All events are under His sovereign providence.

God acts by speaking. He created the world for His glory. He made mankind in His image and gave us responsibility, creativity, and importance. He formed a close and personal bond with humanity through human words. Everything the Triune God created was good.

The most magnificent angel among God's creations became prideful. He desired to replace God and gain glory and honor for himself. The prideful creature rebelled with violence. So, God cast him down from His holy mountain to this world. The names of the angel are Satan, the Devil, and the serpent of old.

Satan caused the original sin by tempting Adam and Eve to disobey God. Their decision to disobey came from their ability to choose whatever they wanted. Disobeying God's rule led to mankind's fall into total depravity. Satan became the ruler of this world. Their disobedience also brought corruption to all the earth through God's curses.

To draw people back into a faithful relationship, God began His redeeming plan. His plan to save humanity from sin was determined before the world began. God the Father established animal sacrifices to teach people that sin results in death. These animal sacrifices served as substitutes for sinners. It eased God's justice and wrath—at least for a while.

God continued to communicate through human words and gave Scripture to mankind. He selected prophets. They provided a special revelation of God for the people, which they spoke and wrote down. God breathed out His Word through the Holy Spirit. He guided His chosen authors to write it in their own styles and voices.

God desires that we know Him through Scripture. He wants us to be obedient to His Word.

Generations after Noah and the flood, God chose Abraham to be His friend. He shared a special bond with Abraham. Abraham wasn't more righteous than others before him, but he had strong faith. He believed God. The Triune God set up the Abrahamic covenant. The sign of this covenant was circumcision, which began years later. God promised to give land to Abraham, as well as a nation of descendants and blessings. God later tested him and viewed him as a righteous man because he kept believing in God.

It took longer than the lives of the patriarchs Abraham, Isaac, Jacob, and Joseph to get to the promised land. Even though it took a long time, they didn't stop believing it would happen. At the end of his life, Joseph prophesied that God would bring Abraham's descendants out of Egypt. They lived in exile, but God promised to take them to a new land. This was the land He had promised to Abraham long ago.

The children of Israel lived in Egypt for about 300 years. During this time, they were in exile and slavery. Their numbers grew to over a million. Under a harsh Pharaoh, their lives were tough. They cried out to the Lord for help. God had pity and sent Moses to rescue them through a very great deliverance pervaded by miracles.

God used Moses to lead the Israelites to the Promised Land. He also established the Mosaic Covenant by giving them laws to follow. The purpose of the Law was to teach the Israelites that sin is offensive, so they must be holy because God is holy.

The descendants of Abraham sinned over and over. God used two corrective measures to deal with the stubborn people. When the descendants were disloyal, He caused them to live in exile. When they were ready to repent and follow Him, God provided rescue.

The Israelites continued to sin often against the Lord on the way to the Promised Land. So, God made them wander for 40 years in the wilderness. After Moses died, the children of Israel entered the Promised Land. This happened under Joshua's leadership around 1406 BC.

About 300 years later, a brave teenage shepherd named David honored God. He did this in front of both the Israelites and their enemy. With strong faith in God, he defeated a killer giant. Bringing honor to God's name was the typical manner of David; although he did sin, he also repented. God called David "a man after His own heart."

God made David king over the Israelites and instituted the Davidic Covenant. He made unconditional promises to David: 1) He would give David a great name and peace from his enemies. 2) He would settle the Israelites in their own land. 3) He would create an everlasting kingdom through David's line. His line led to the Messiah, Jesus, who came about 1,000 years later.

The prophets shared a critical key message in Scripture: sin leads to death or punishment. This includes exile for those who offend God. Sinners lose a close relationship with Him. They face a life filled with brokenness and hardship. The prophets made many appeals for God's people to repent and turn back to Him in obedience. They gave the Israelites literature to help them gain wisdom, too. This way, they would know how to live in ways that please God.

The Israelites lived in exile for much of their history. Their disobedience was frequent and lasted for many hundreds of years. Too many times to list here, enemies have exiled God's people. One good thing about exile is that it encourages repentance. It also brings refreshing times when the moment is right. God's prophets encouraged the people by revealing that a new covenant was coming. Father God would bring a future King to lead a righteous and everlasting kingdom.

God sent the prophet Malachi to the rebellious Israelites

around 450-430 BC. About 400 years later, prophecies from the Old Testament about the Messiah started coming true. The first major prophecy was that a virgin would give birth to a baby in Bethlehem. This baby was a descendant of Abraham and King David. The covenants God made with these men hundreds of years before were fulfilled in Jesus. This baby grew to be a man who never sinned. He taught the people with divine wisdom and performed countless healings and miracles. Each book of the Bible contains subtle references to the Messiah, Jesus, the coming King. Over 400 verses in the Old Testament prophesied of His first coming, and all have been fulfilled.

God was Jesus's divine Father, and Mary, a teenage Jewish girl, was His mother. This Son of Man had both divine and human natures. But hateful, unbelieving people tortured and crucified Jesus for reasons based on pride and disbelief. Jesus rose back to life three days after dying on the cross. Over 500 people saw Him after His resurrection; some also saw His ascension to heaven. And there will be a second coming of Jesus. Over 1800 Bible prophecy references point to Jesus' second coming, and the vast majority have been fulfilled. We are getting down to the wire, folks.

God established a new covenant through Jesus. This started with His death, then His resurrection, glorification, and ascension. More prophecy came true at Pentecost when God gave the Holy Spirit to believers who repented. That happened about 2000 years ago. God fulfilled His promise: *"I will give you a new heart and a new spirit. I will take away your heart of stone and give you a heart of flesh. And I will put My Spirit in you and move you to follow My decrees and be careful to keep My laws."* (Ezekiel 36:26-27)

God has established His everlasting Kingdom. To clarify, the new substitute sacrifice for sinners is the perfect Lamb of God, Messiah Jesus. He chose to die as a sacrifice to pay the debt to God for mankind's sins. Those who repent and believe in Christ receive forgiveness for all their sins. They can then commune with Him while abiding in Him. So, there is no longer a need for animal sacrifices to satisfy God's justice and wrath.

The Church began at Pentecost. That's when Christ Jesus baptized repentant believers with the Holy Spirit. The Holy Spirit comes to live in every believer, causing them to become reborn. He gives power and special gifts to help serve and strengthen the body of Christ. Christ is the head. God has given the Church apostles, prophets, evangelists, pastors, and teachers. He has also provided a structure that includes elders, deacons, and members. The Spirit gives gifts to each member of Christ's body. These gifts serve different purposes based on how the Lord wants to use each believer. He has given many gifts, including wisdom, knowledge, faith, and healing. Other gifts are miraculous powers, prophecy, discerning spirits, and speaking in other languages.

Some differing opinions exist on which gifts people still exercise in our modern day. Still, the Spirit gives important gifts. All believers should use their gifts from God. This is for His glory, to love and serve others, and to share the gospel of Christ. The Church's mission is clear: followers of Christ are citizens of heaven. They must live as cultural exiles on earth.

As time passes, more Bible prophecies are being fulfilled. This shows that Christ's return to earth is nearer. Followers of Jesus must spread the good news of His redemption to all nations; then the end will come.

The Church continues its work on earth, but many deceivers will claim to be the Messiah. There will be wars and rumors of wars. Frequent earthquakes and severe famines will happen. People will face great troubles, and the love of many will grow cold.

Then comes the Great Tribulation. People everywhere will then suffer more severe hardships than ever before. This will be worse than anything since the beginning of time. Sin and hatred for God will grow. This will lead to the Triune God's anger and the delivery of justice.

Many Christians believe the Bible teaches Christ will remove His Church from the world before the Great Tribulation. These believe it will be a supernatural event known as the Rapture, but opinions vary about the timing. Some people wonder if it will happen at all. Others wonder if it will be before or after the Great Tribulation or in the middle of that terrible time.

The Bible says that after the Great Tribulation, Jesus will return to earth the second time. He will defeat evil and confine Satan for a while. He will reign on earth, and there will be peace for 1,000 years.

Then God will release Satan once more to deceive the nations. The Lord God will be checking the apostasy of people who say they love King Jesus. But do they? Their actions will tell God where their hearts are. Peace will end with the final battle at Armageddon in northern Israel. It will be the final, catastrophic battle; then Satan will be confined to Hell.

Following this event will be the Great White Throne Judgment. The Triune God will bring every act to judgment—whether good or evil. Those who have turned away from Christ will endure eternal punishment. When people reject Jesus, they show they love sin—not Him.

During judgment time, God will reward Christians according to their service and lives.

In King Jesus's heavenly kingdom, we will have responsibilities. There will be no sin, hunger, thirst, sickness, tears, pain, or death. Instead, we will experience joy and share love as we serve others and glorify our God every way we can—and we will love it! The Church, including Abraham's believing descendants, will realize God's plan for humanity forevermore.

God wants your attention.
There is something He wants you to do.

AUTHOR'S NOTES:

My hope for this book is that it will encourage people to realize God is still working. Perceive His glory by drawing near to God through Christ Jesus, the Lord, and He will draw near to you. He wants you to know and believe that He notices every person's life, cares, and is participating. He has purpose and is working out His plans. You must trust in His Word and hold on to faith.

Read the Bible with a heart desiring truth. Remember that Satan and his influencers twist the Bible's teachings to fit your selfish desires, not God's will. Their desire is to steal, kill, and destroy you.

The beautiful artwork used on this book cover was discovered at Adobe Stock Art, www.stock.adobe.com.

Suggested Reading
and Resources:

The Holy Bible by God through about 40 different authors

The Holiness of God by Dr. R.C. Sproul

The Gospel According to Jesus by Dr. John MacArthur Jr.

God's Devil by Dr. Erwin Lutzer

Evidence That Demands a Verdict by Josh & Sean McDowell

Science proves Christian faith: *https://reasons.org*

Worshipful Christian radio: *https://khcb.org*

Christian programing and current events: *https://afr.net*

Help for the family: *https://www.focusonthefamily.com*

Christian commentary: *https://wretched.org*

True life testimonies: https://*unshackled.org*

Messianic Prophecies: *https://www.hopeoftheworld.org*

NOTICE: The ministries noted above are not aware of this author, so they may or may not support the concept of this book.